This book is dedicated to
John, Paul, George, and Ringo
...and dreamers everywhere.

Once Upon A Time In Liverpool

**WORDS BY
JUDITH KRISTEN**

**ART BY
ERIC CASH**

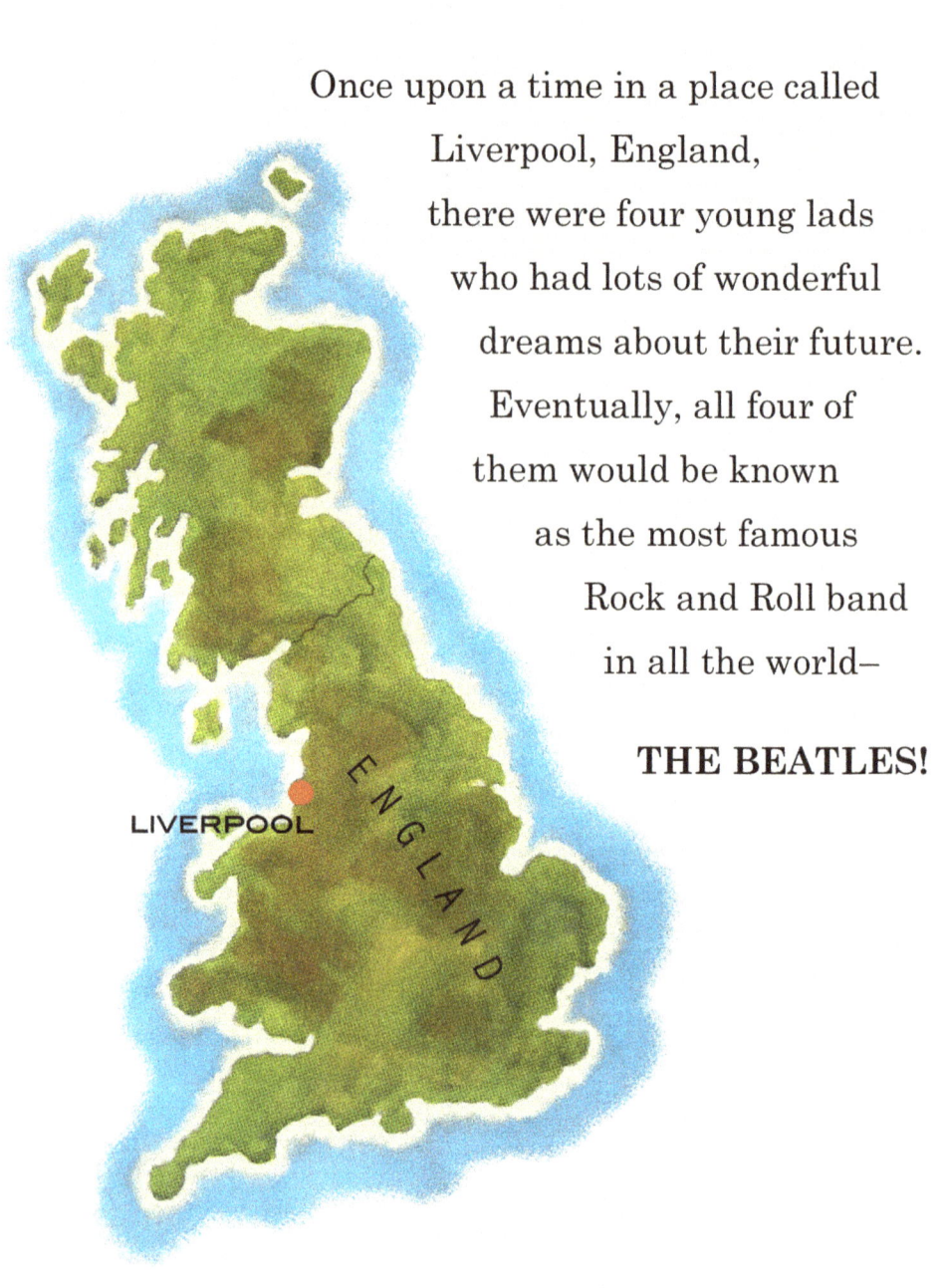

Once upon a time in a place called
Liverpool, England,
there were four young lads
who had lots of wonderful
dreams about their future.
Eventually, all four of
them would be known
as the most famous
Rock and Roll band
in all the world—

THE BEATLES!

It's good to dream!

One of those four boys was named John Lennon. John was born on October 9th, 1940.

John is one of the older members of the group. John was also a natural-born leader and formed the group.

John was funny and well liked. He loved to draw and write stories when he was just a lad, and he was very good at it!

John's father's name was Alfred. Alfred was a merchant seaman and was seldom at home with his family. John's mother's name was Julia. Julia was a woman who loved life. She even knew how to play a ukulele! Sadly, Julia died when John was just a teenager.

Because of his early family troubles, John went to live with his Aunt Mimi.
The lovely home that John lived in with Mimi was called Mendips.

Isn't it fun to have a house with it's own name?

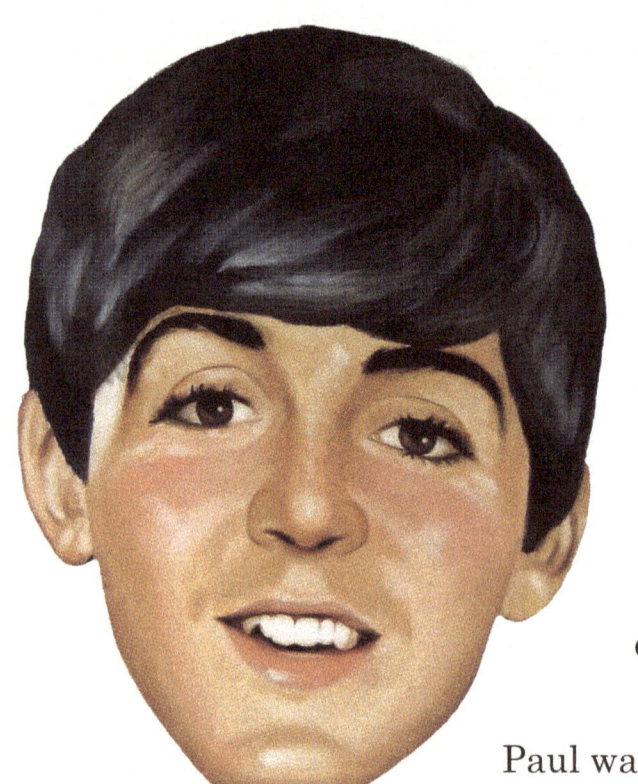

Another one of those four young lads was born on June 18th, 1942. His name was James Paul McCartney– but everyone called him Paul.

Paul was really friendly, and like John, was very well-liked.

Paul was the second boy to join the group. He was left-handed, and could play the guitar really well. He was also very smart, and did well in school.

Paul's father's name was James. He was a hard-working cotton salesman. He loved to play music and to read as did Paul. Paul's mother Mary died when he was a teenager like John. Paul had a younger brother named Michael, and their dad loved them both very much.

Even though it was difficult for James at times to be a single dad, Paul and Michael grew up in a wonderfully kind and loving family.

Weren't they lucky to have such a nice dad?

Not far from Paul's home lived a lanky, shaggy-haired young fellow with a charming smile, who eventually became one of The Beatles as well. His name was George Harrison. George was born on February 25th, 1943.

George was a little quiet, and had lots of friends. He was the youngest boy in the group. He also loved to play the guitar.

George's mother's name was Louise. His father's name was Harold. George had two older brothers, Harry, Peter, and a beautiful sister named Louise.

They all lived in a tiny two-bedroom home, but there was enough love in that house to fill a mansion. George's mother was a very happy homemaker.
George's dad was a bus driver.
The big green bus he drove was the bus Number 81.

I like to ride on a bus.
Don't you?

The last of the four lads from Liverpool to join the group, was raised in a very poor section of the city called the Dingle. His name was Richard Starkey, but his friends called him Ritchie. When he was older he changed his name to Ringo. Because he liked the sound of it, he wore lots of rings.

Ringo was born on July 7th, 1940. He was the oldest member of the group. Ringo was very sick as a child, but he learned to play the drums and that made him feel better.

Ringo's mother's name was Elsie. She loved her son with all of her heart. Even though Ringo was sickly when he was a little boy, his family took good care of him.

Ringo never knew much about his birth father, but he had a stepdad named Harry who loved him as if he were his own.

Even through all of his childhood hardships, Ringo kept his wonderful sense of humor and his spirited good nature.

Ringo's family was poor, but they were rich in all the ways that really mattered.

All four lads grew up and did the
things we all do as children
and young teenagers.
They went to school, enjoyed
the company of their friends,
went to the movies, rode their
bicycles, and drank lots of tea
(tea is the most popular drink
in England) and they
visited the seaside.

But most of all,
they loved to
listen to music!

When the four of them were young teenagers the popular music in Liverpool was called "Skiffle". Skiffle music was a very different kind of music. Skiffle bands used lots of unusual instruments: washboards, tea chest basses, old drinking jugs, cigar box fiddles, comb-and-paper kazoos, as well as some regular instruments such as guitars and banjos.

Do you think you would like to play in a Skiffle band? I think that would be LOTS of fun!

Their most favorite
musicians were
Elvis Presley,
Carl Perkins,
Buddy Holly, and
Little Richard.

U.K.

Do you like Rock and Roll music?
I bet you do!

John Lennon was so inspired by Rock and Roll that he started his own group called the Quarrymen. One day John's group was asked to perform at the Woolton Parish Church Garden Fete in Liverpool– and happily they said yes!
The date was July 6th, 1957.

Paul McCartney was in the audience that day and he really liked what he heard. He enjoyed the music, but he especially liked John's style, charm, and sense of humor.
That very day in the nearby church auditorium a mutual friend, named Ivan Vaughn, introduced Paul to John. John liked Paul straight away.
He was a good guitar player, a great singer, and a handsome lad as well!
So of course, Paul became a band member– and John's very dear friend.

George Harrison was also a very dear friend of Paul's—
and a pretty good guitar player to boot!
George auditioned to be part of the band as the
three lads rode through Liverpool on the top
level of a double-decker bus.
George played a song called "Raunchy" on his guitar
for John, and John loved it!
Then of course, George became a band member too!

So, at that time there were three very good friends who were all three wonderful guitar players and fabulous singers as well. That was great, but they needed someone to play the drums.

Soon, another young boy joined the band and became their drummer. He was a very good-looking lad from Liverpool. His name was Pete Best.

Just about that same time, a school friend of John's also became a member of the group. His name was Stuart Sutcliffe. Stu was an extremely creative and talented artist- and he even played a bass guitar!

In what ways are you creative?

The band went through several names before finally settling on the one we all know today. After the Quarrymen, they were called: The Nurk Twins, The Blackjacks, Johnny and the Moondogs, Silver Beats, The Beatals, and The Silver Beetles.

Then one night, as legend has it, John had a very strange dream and it made him decide to change the band's name one last time. As John later recalled, "A man appeared on a flaming pie and said, 'From now on you are Beatles with an A'"

So, there they were: John, Paul, George, Stuart and Pete– now called **The Beatles**!

It took The Beatles quite a few years of very hard work to become a success, even in their own hometown. They traveled all around England and even far, far away to play in a city called Hamburg, Germany. They loved Germany and Germany loved The Beatles! The lads played in many clubs there— sometimes for twelve hours a day, seven days a week!

They loved what they were doing, but it was still a LOT of work and with very little pay. There was even a time when they felt so discouraged that they all decided to call it quits, and for a few weeks they did! But, that didn't work out very well. They were miserable without their music, without their dreams, and without each other. They knew that being part of a Rock and Roll band was what they were meant to do, and lucky for all of us, the music won out!

The Beatles were a band once again— and the world was about to become a much happier place.

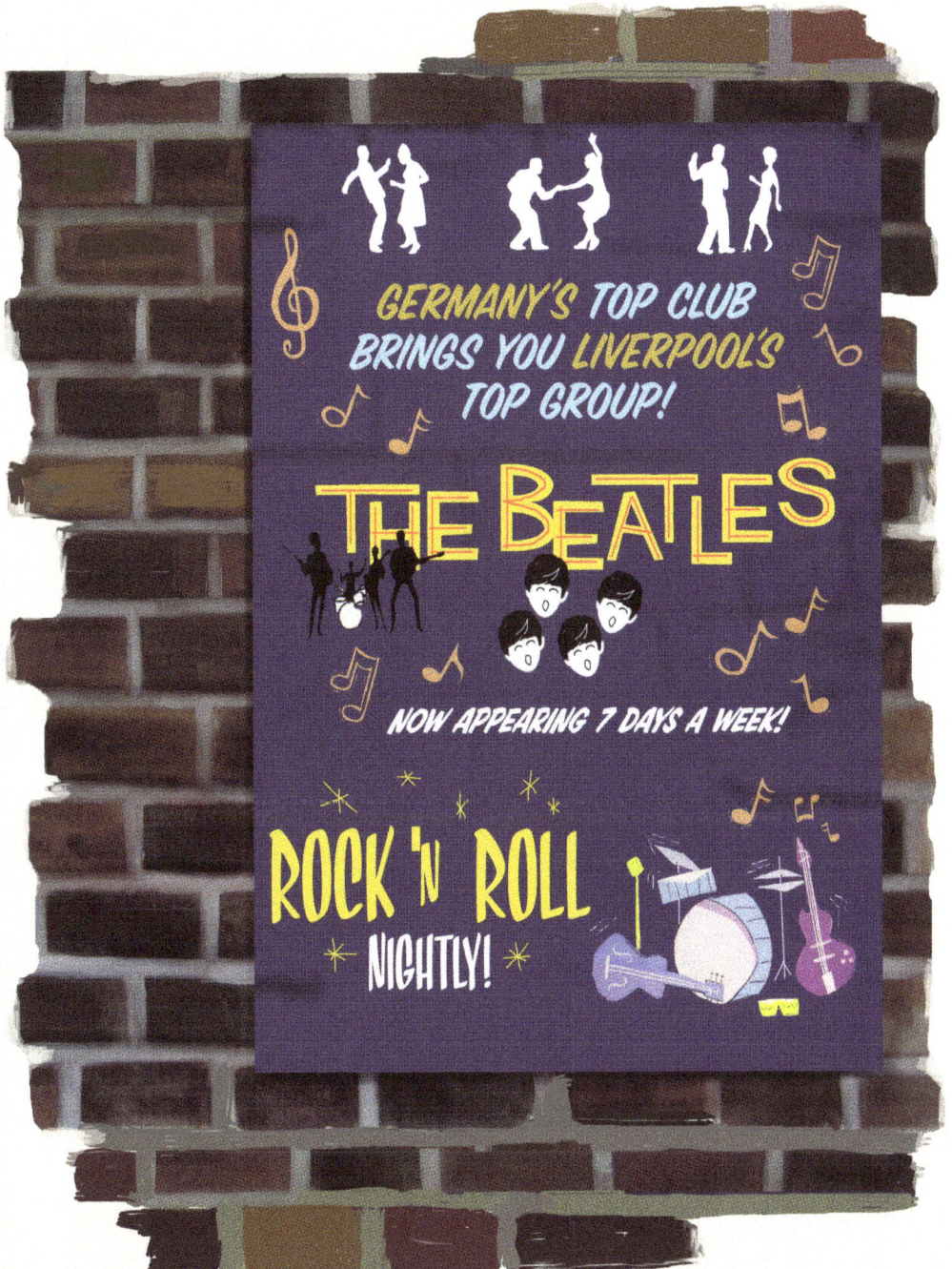

As time moved on certain things changed. Sadly, Stuart passed away in Hamburg at the age of 21. As for Pete Best? John, Paul, and George felt like he was no longer right for their particular sound, and so Pete was asked to leave the group.

Since Ringo Starr was already a well-known drummer in Liverpool, and because his personality fit the group perfectly, he was asked to become their official drummer, and in the end, as you know, that worked out just fine.

Soon, their long Hamburg days and nights were over, and all that hard-work began to pay off.
Back in their homeland, their dreams were starting to come true.
By then, The Beatles were so popular in Liverpool, that they played the Cavern Club 292 times!

Now that's really popular!!!

In fact, The Beatles became
so popular all over Great Britain
that they were asked to appear at
the Royal Variety Performance.

The event took place on November 4th, 1963
at the Prince of Wales Theatre in London
in the presence of the Queen Mother and
her daughter Princess Margaret.

Can you imagine that?!
How exciting!

Do you think the Queen Mother and the Princess were Beatles fans?

Not long after their Royal Performance, some people in America heard about The Beatles and the lads were asked to come to the United States to play their music on television. The program they played on was called the Ed Sullivan Show. It was the most popular show in America at that time.

And on February 9th, 1964, 73 million people tuned in to watch The Beatles perform five of their most popular songs! That was the largest number of people who EVER watched the same television show all at the same time!

Teenage girls LOVED The Beatles, but they were popular with teenage boys as well. In fact lots of adults way back then liked them too! Soon those four young lads from Liverpool were loved the world over.
Their music filled our hearts, and we danced and smiled, and sang along, every time we heard one of their records play!
From then on, as they say, the rest is history!

So here we are, many, many years beyond those times, when four young lads from Liverpool dreamed dreams, that somehow, came true for all of us.

John, Paul, George, and Ringo–
The Beatles,
gave the world it's
Happily Ever After

After all, isn't that the best way
to end a story?

It sure is.

Once Upon A Time In Liverpool
Copyright 2020 by Eric Cash & Judy Kristen
All rights reserved

2 4 6 8 10 9 7 5 3 1

ISBN 978-1-946182-07-4

Written by Judith Kristen
www.judithkristen.com
www.adatewithabeatle.com

Illustrated & Cover design by Eric Cash
www.ericcashillustrations.com

Published by
Debe Ink

www.debeink.com

www.ingramcontent.com/pod-product-compliance
Lightning Source LLC
Chambersburg PA
CBHW041301240426

43661CB00010B/975